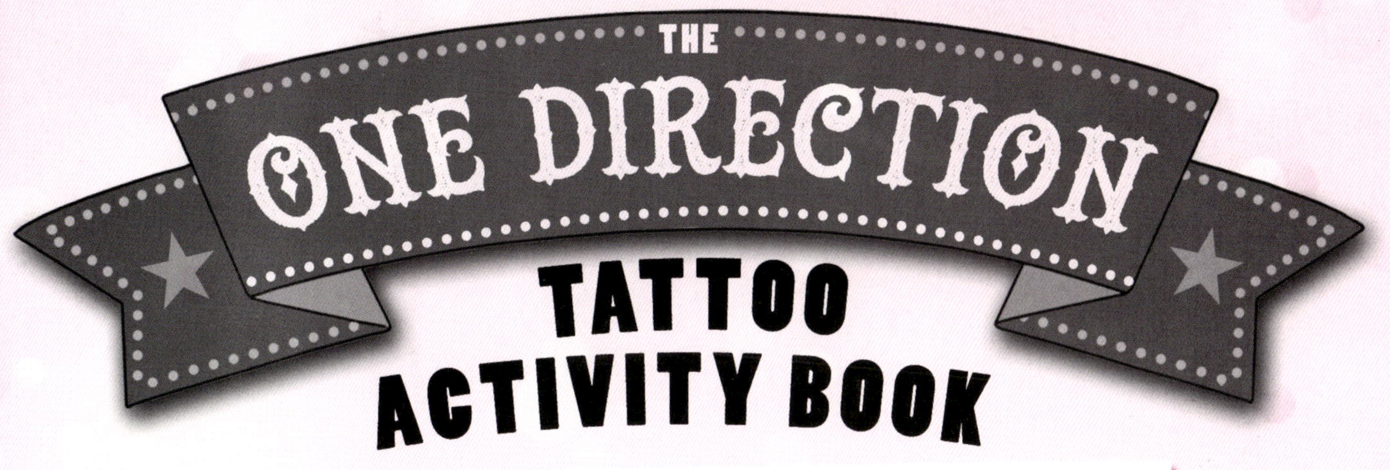

THE ONE DIRECTION TATTOO ACTIVITY BOOK

With 24 Amazing Temporary Tattoos to Wear and Share

BARRON'S

First edition for the United States and Canada published in 2014
by Barron's Educational Series, Inc.

Published in 2014 by Carlton Books Limited
An imprint of the Carlton Publishing Group
20 Mortimer Street, London W1T 3JW

All inquiries should be addressed to:
Barron's Educational Series, Inc.
250 Wireless Boulevard
Hauppauge, NY 11788
www.barronseduc.com

ISBN: 978-1-4380-0588-1

Product conforms to all applicable CPSC and CPSIA 2008 standards.
No lead or phthalate hazard.

Date of Manufacture: August 2014
Manufactured by: RRD South China, Dongguan, China

Printed in China

9 8 7 6 5 4 3 2 1

Picture Credits
All photographs kindly supplied by Rex Features & Shutterstock with the exception of the following:

pg 1 & 3 Jon Kopaloff/FilmMagic/Getty Images, pg 2 (center) FOX via Getty Images & pg 27 (bottom right) Erik Pendzich/Demotix/Corbis

Every effort has been made to acknowledge correctly and contact the source and/or copyright holder of each picture and Carlton Books Limited apologizes for any unintentional errors or omissions, which will be corrected in future editions of this book.

With 24 Amazing Temporary Tattoos to Wear and Share

One Direction have taken the world by storm with their catchy songs and gorgeous looks. Now you can get even closer to them and cement your status as their number one fan by covering your arms in these removable tattoos!

TOP TATTOOS

Everyone knows the boys love their tattoos; now you can follow their style without any pain, by wearing and sharing these removable tattoos!

Show your love for Louis with his picture on your arm, share Harry's styles (get it?!) with a bird or a butterfly, copy Zayn's "ZAP!" or try a pretty feather like Liam. But don't worry—even if you're like Niall and prefer to avoid the ink, you can just try a tattoo for a day and then safely remove it! Find the instructions on the back of your tattoo sheet.

TATTOO TIPS

- Choose somewhere discreet for your first tattoos. That way, you can cover it up if you need to, and then give all your friends a sneak peek.
- Make sure your skin is clean and grease-free before applying the tattoo.
- When you wait for the tattoo to bind to your skin, try to move as little as possible.
- Leave the tattoo to dry completely before you touch it or put clothing over it.

WHOSE TATTOO

Can you match each tattoo to its owner?

1 ....

2 ....

3 ....

4 ....

5 ....

6 ....

7 ....

8 ....

9 ....

10 ....

Find the answers on page 40

INK-REDIBLE!

The heart on Harry's left bicep isn't some lovey dovey graphic—it's an anatomically correct picture complete with valves and ventricles!

Zayn, Harry, and Louis have more than 20 tattoos each.

Zayn's spiderweb tattoo is a tribute to his cartoon superhero, Spider-Man.

The feather on Liam's arm is to remind him of his beloved granny.

Niall is the only band member without a tattoo—although he did get a fake fern on his wrist when they toured in New Zealand!

All of the guys (except Niall, obviously) have matching screw tattoos on their ankle.

MEET THE BAND

Harry is the youngest in the band, and was only 16 when he took part in the *X Factor* auditions.

Formed in 2010 after finishing third in series seven of the U.K.'s X Factor, One Direction have broken world records in their meteoric rise to fame. They are the first British group EVER to go straight to number 1 in the U.S. with their debut album. That same album, *Up All Night*, sold over one million copies in the first week. Along with two more albums, the band released their film *This Is Us*, giving their devoted fans even more insight into what fun-loving and friendly guys they really are. The movie only went on to became the biggest-grossing documentary of the year—of course!

Zayn nearly didn't make it into the band, as he pulled out at the auditions stage because of nerves and stage fright.

Niall has described the band as "five singing idiots." Pretty successful idiots, hey?!

KISS YOU

Play this game at your next 1D party (it's a little sad if you're caught playing it on your own). You'll need to choose a large poster of the band—one that you don't mind getting covered in kisses! Take turns layering on loads of lipstick and then tie a scarf around your eyes as a blindfold. Someone shouts out a nomination for which band member you have to kiss. Aim to plant a smacker as close to his lips as you possibly can!

What do you call cheese that isn't yours?

Nacho cheese!

Liam is the down-to-earth one—they call him Daddy Directioner because he looks after them all.

Louis is the oldes[t] band member but sees himself as the most immature, and the joker of the group.

NAME: Liam ....

HOMETOWN: ....

NAME: Harry ....

HOMETOWN: ....

NAME: Louis ....

HOMETOWN: ....

NAME: Niall ....

HOMETOWN: ....

NAME: Zayn ....

HOMETOWN: ....

MATCHMAKING

Do you know each band member's full name and where they were born? Try and write the boys' correct middle and last names and their hometowns in the spaces provided.

Find the answers on page 40

BEST BAND EVER

Of course! So here's a bonus double pic for you—but see if you can spot ten differences between the two.

Find the answers on page 40

EVERYTHING ABOUT YOU

How well do you feel you know these five superstars? Have you watched the movie so many times you can lip-synch with the sound turned down? Do you know what they're up to and where they are at every waking moment? Could you call Harry's mom and let her know when he'll be home next, please?

TELL ME A LIE

Here's a test for you—which One Direction-er is fibbing?

Zayn: I had never been on a plane before I was in the band.

Louis: I sleepwalk!

Harry: I set my hair on fire onstage in Chicago.

Niall: I broke my toe by dropping my laptop on it!

Liam: I auditioned on *X Factor* in 2008.

WHERE WE ARE

Take a look at this map of the world. The boys have played gigs in all of the places marked with a star. Can you match the clues to each city?

It's cold in the Andes: pack a beanie!

No.

This Asian capital is famous for its temples—and its nightlife!

No.

Time for some Florida fun!

No.

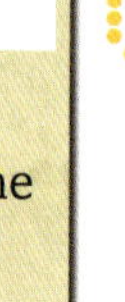

First stop—Niagara Falls. Almost as awesome as 1D!

No.

Not NZ's capital, but its largest city

No.

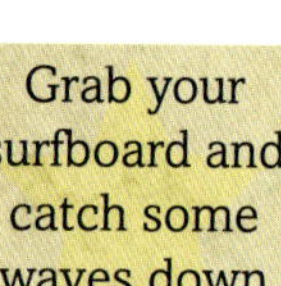

An Irish venue close to Niall's heart

No.

Grab your surfboard and catch some waves down under!

No.

SCENT SATIONAL

The 1D boys aren't the only ones who can launch their own perfumes, you know. You can make your own signature scent by picking your fave flowers (by smell, not the ones that look prettiest)—remove the stems and chop up the petals. Soak them in water for around 20 minutes and then add a teaspoon of warm water and a teaspoon of salt. Stir and smell. If you like the result, store it in a small, airtight bottle or jar. Don't forget to design your own label!

BEST SONG EVER

Put on some tunes and play this sing-along game with your craziest friends. Take turns choosing a track. Turn it up and start to sing. One of your friends then turns the volume down while you carry on singing your heart out. Turn the sound back up and see if you've stayed in time—or strayed horribly out of sync!

STORY OF MY LIFE

Who is being described here?

I have an older sister named Gemma. I won the "Best Look Award" at the MTV VMAs in 2013. I was born in 1994.

....

Find the answer on page 40

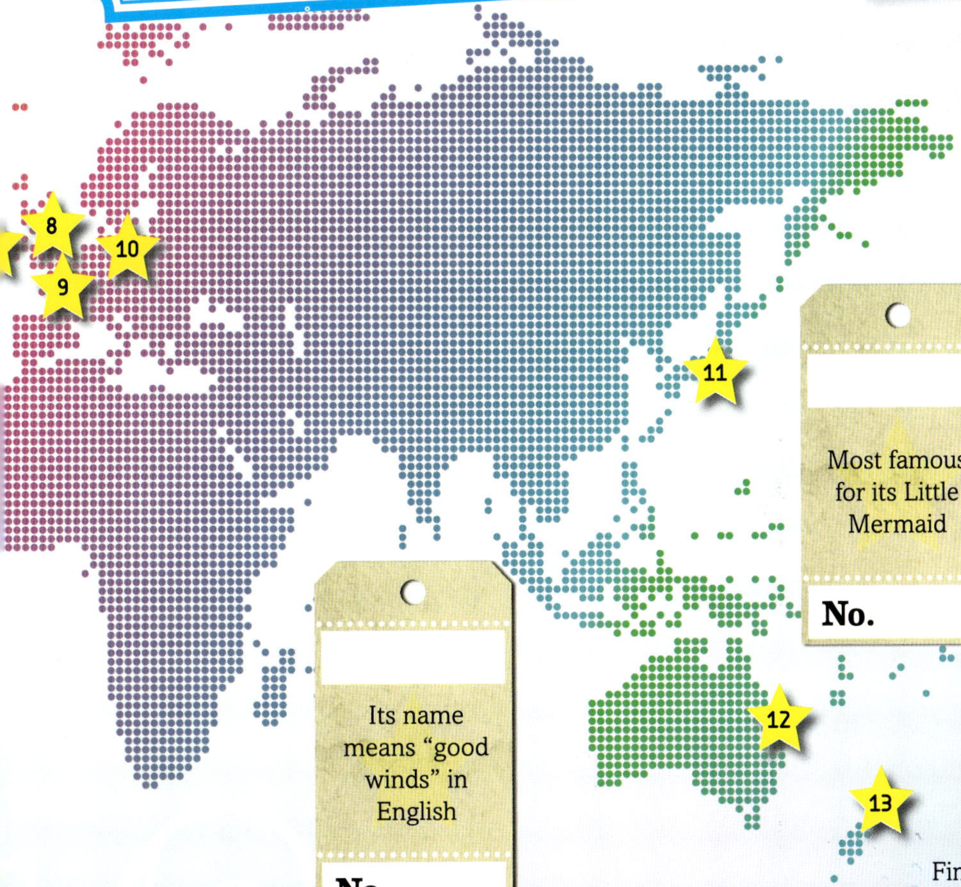

8 9 10 11 12 13

Chance to pick up an Aztec tattoo design?
No.

Carnival, parties, great Brazilian beaches—what's not to love?
No.

Most famous for its Little Mermaid
No.

The city closest to Harry's hometown
No.

If you've a head for heights you can climb the Eiffel Tower
No.

Its name means "good winds" in English
No.

Find the answers on page 40

He's the oldest member of the band, so let's meet him first.

Louis Tomlinson

BIRTHPLACE: Doncaster (England)

BIRTH DATE: December 24, 1991

ASTROLOGICAL SIGN: Capricorn

PARENTS: Mom Johannah; dad Troy; stepdad Mark

HOBBIES: Soccer, surfing, skateboarding

LIKES TO LISTEN TO: Robbie Williams, The Fray, The Killers

FAVE COLOR: Dark red

FAVE COUNTRY: France

LOOK OUT FOR: His signature stripes! He's often seen in striped tees and sweatshirts

THINGS THAT MAKE HIM GO "MMMM": Marmite on toast

mmmm!

THINGS THAT MAKE HIM GO "OOGH": Baked beans, noisy eaters

TOP TATTOOS: Suits of cards on his wrist; Pacman; Tic-Tac-Toe; "It is what it is" on his chest; bird on right arm; and lots more!

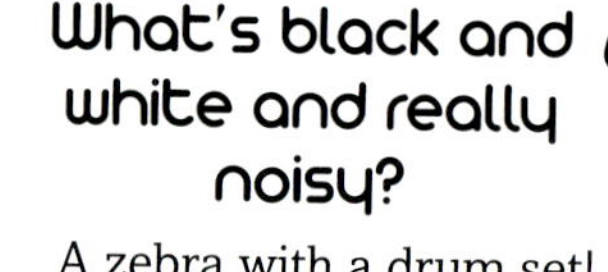

FEELING ODD

Louis is happiest when he's with the others, but here he is, all alone. Which of the Louis pics is the odd one out, though?

Find the answer on page 40

FACE FACTS

So, you think you're the world's biggest Louis fan? Show your allegiance with some top-notch face paints to make you stand out from the crowd. Louis's simple tattoos are easy as pie to copy with an eyeliner pencil or proper face paint.

CALL ME ... LOU?

Louis's bandmates have given him lots of nicknames, but which ones of these are made up?

Hughey

Robbo

Boobear

Mr. Pinkerton

Tommo

Brian

Lolly Bolly

Lou

Luigi

Find the answers on page 40

DID YOU KNOW?

★ Louis was born Louis Troy Austin but took his stepfather's name when he was little.

★ He had acting jobs before he joined the band, and made a handful of TV appearances.

★ A talented soccer player, Louis was signed by Doncaster Rovers FC and wears the number 28 shirt whenever he is able to make an appearance.

RIGHT NOW

STORY OF MY LIFE

Who is this?
I lived with my dad after my parents split up. I sang in the school choir. I'm left-handed but I play guitar right-handed.

....

Find the answer (above an below) o pag 4

Right now, they're the hottest thing in pop. Three best-selling albums and there's no sign of them stopping! In addition to breaking records for their chart successes, One Direction is also receiving recognition at award ceremonies. Best British Video and Global Success awards at the 2014 Brit Awards; Best Pop at the MTV EMA Awards; Best Song of the Summer (Best Song Ever) at the 2013 MTV Music Awards; and all nine of the Teen Choice Awards they were nominated for in 2012!

NAME THAT TUNE

What words fill in the blanks in these song titles?

1. **Tell me a** .... joke/story/lie
2. **Better than** .... cake/words/ever
3. **Change my** .... mind/socks/friends
4. **Through the** .... keyhole/dark/mirror
5. **They don't know about** .... us/Liam/anything
6. **Back for** .... good/more/you
7. **Everything about** .... you/the girl/everyone
8. **Don't forget where you** .... live/belong/left your hat

Find the answers on page 40

WRITTEN IN THE CARDS

Let the cards predict your future...! Take the Jacks out of an ordinary pack of cards and lay them face up in a row. Ask a friend to name each Jack after her fave band member (sorry, you can only have four—it's a toughie!). Your friend must shuffle the remaining cards and choose one to keep for later, unseen.

Now she has to ask questions for the cards to answer: Which of the boys will she meet first? Which of them will think she's gorgeous? Who will ask her out? Which of them will send her a valentine? For each of her questions, deal the cards onto the Jacks, one by one, until a suit matches. So if the fourth card is a heart, and is dealt onto the Jack of hearts, that 1Der is the answer.

Keep going until the cards are used up, and then reveal your friend's mystery card. That one depicts which of the boys is her true love!

ONE DIRECTION

Follow the arrows from start to finish in the direction they are pointing. You should be able to find a way through the grid, passing all five 1Ders on your journey.

START

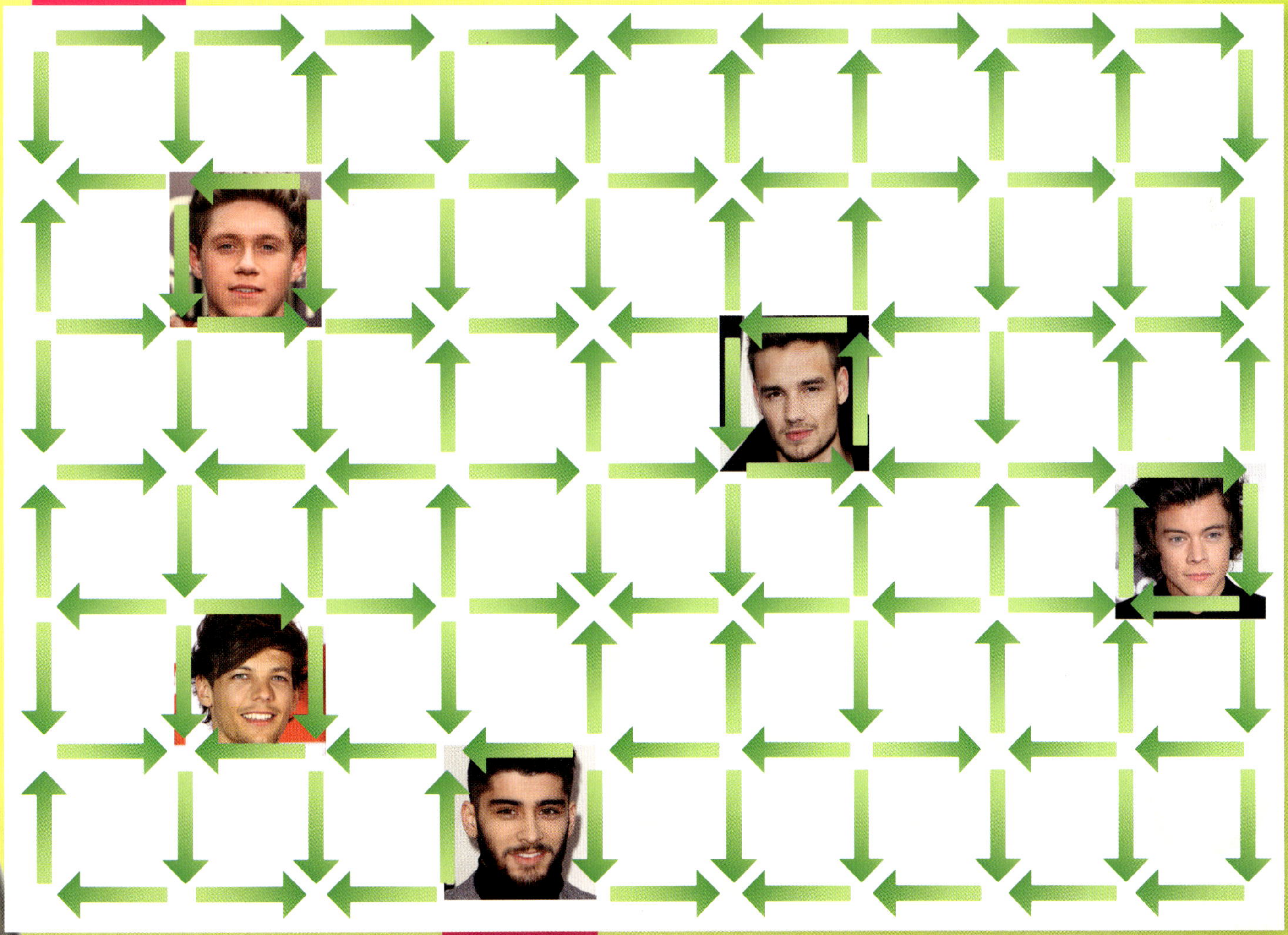

FINISH

Find the answer on page 40

He says he's the shy one—let's find out more about him.

Zayn Malik

BIRTHPLACE: Bradford (England)

BIRTH DATE: January 12, 1993

ASTROLOGICAL SIGN: Capricorn

PARENTS: Mom Tricia (short for Patricia); dad Yaser

HOBBIES: Drawing, reading

LIKES TO LISTEN TO: Michael Jackson, *NSYNC, Bruno Mars

FAVE COLOR: Black

FAVE COUNTRY: Ireland

LOOK OUT FOR: His cool hair, whether it's big and bouffed or dyed and flipped

mmmm!

THINGS THAT MAKE HIM GO "MMMM": Chicken, samosas

THINGS THAT MAKE HIM GO "OOGH": People who chew (loudly) with their mouth open

TOP TATTOOS: ZAP! on his right arm; yin/yang on his wrist; crossed fingers; microphone on his inner arm, and crown on his chest

ZAYN'S MAZE

What's Zayn's favorite animal? Find a way through the maze to find out!

....

Find the answer on page 40

START

GORILLA

DOLPHINS

LION

HORSE

PUPPY LOVE

How much of a Zayn addict are you? Do you know which of these was NOT one of his pets when he was younger?

Lily ◯
Lolo ◯
Tonto ◯
Tyson ◯

Find the answer on page 40

What kind of car does a farmer drive?

A corn-vertible!

DID YOU KNOW?

★ His name means "beautiful king" in Arabic. It's actually spelled Zain but he changed it when he joined the band.

★ Zayn has created his own superstition of having to brush his teeth before he goes on stage.

★ When he was eight, he had a crazy dream that he was being chased by a giant Power Ranger…

The 1D boys say, over and over again, that they love their fans. They do their very best to interact with them on social media, and to keep the Directioners up to date on what they're doing—even if it's just kicking back and having some down time. After all, if their fans are happy, the boys are happy, right? How many of the 1D guys are you following?

MORE THAN THIS

Put your brain to the test: how many new words, with three letters or more, can you make out of this album title? Here's one to get you started.

MIDNIGHT MEMORIES

Heroes ....

....

....

....

....

....

....

....

Find the answers on page 40

STORY OF MY LIFE

Who is talking here?

I have two older sisters, Ruth and Nicola. I studied music technology at college. I was born in 1993.

....

Find the answer on page 40

IN PIECES

Gah! Don't you just hate it when a piece of your jigsaw puzzle is missing? Luckily, Harry has found some pieces behind the sofa. Which one do you need to finish the puzzle?

Find the answer on page 40

Why do gorillas have big nostrils?

Becasue they have big fingers!

LIVE PERFORMANCE

The boys are singing their hearts out, as always! Can you spot five differences between these two shots? Color the boys' outfits, too.

Find the answers on page 40

Who said what? Draw a line to match each of the 1D boys to the correct quote.

"We're not perfect, we're not clean cut. We're trying to be ourselves."

"If it were legal, I'd marry food."

"My trademark saying is probably 'VAS HAPPENIN?!'"

"My sister used to call me Cheesy Head because I loved these cheesy crisps."

"I hope that I'd still be touring with One Direction in ten years' time. I love this job so much—if you need to call it a job."

Find the answers on page 40

HANGING AROUND

Which member of the band is taking time out—and what's he doing? Connect-the-dots to find out.

Find the answer on page 40

FOLLOWING FASHION

Harry's style is so super cool. Which of these shirts should you buy to get one exactly the same as his?

Find the answer on page 40

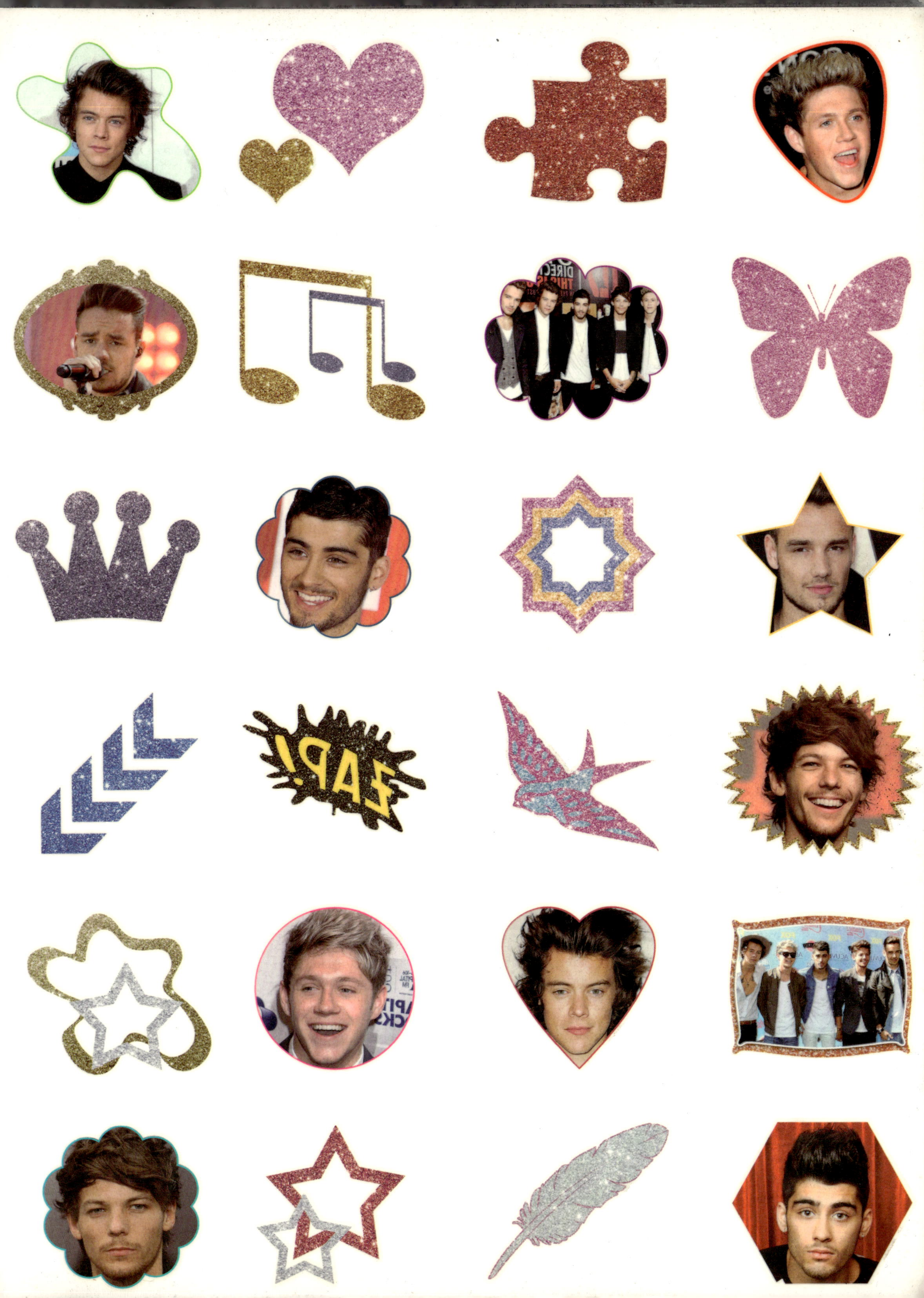
ZAP!

How to apply your tattoo

1 Make sure your skin is clean and dry.
2 Cut out the tattoo you wish to apply.
3 Peel off the plastic top sheet.
4 Place the tattoo face down on your skin and press firmly.
5 Wet the back of the tattoo with a damp sponge or cloth.
6 Wait for 30 seconds.
7 Carefully slide off the backing paper.
8 Rinse with water and let dry.
9 Tattoo lasts for three to five days.

Removal

To remove your tattoo, rub the tattoo gently with baby oil.

Tattoo safety information.

Barron's Educational Series, Inc.
250 Wireless Boulevard, Hauppauge, New York 11788

JFMAMJ ASOND/14/7258-01, Printed in Dongguan, China

Date of manufacture: July 2014
Manufacturer: Wintai Technology Co. Ltd.
Address of manufacturer: Huiyang, Huizhou, Guangdong, China.

Batch: 20140718

Product function: removable temporary tattoos.

Tattoo ingredients: Polyvinyl Acetate, 54%; Water (Aqua), 44%; Titanium Dioxide, 0.5%; D&C Black No. 2, 0.3%; FD&C Blue No. 1 Aluminium Lake, 0.3%; FD&C Yellow No. 5 Aluminium Lake, 0.3%; FD&C Yellow No. 6 Aluminium Lake, 0.3%; D&C Red No. 7 Lake, 0.3%.

Warning: not suitable for children under 36 months due to small parts. Choking hazard.

Best used before the end of July 2015.

Warning! Do not apply on lips or around the eyes. If the product causes irritation, wash the skin immediately. If symptoms continue, seek medical advice.Eczema-type reactions could potentially occur among users who have been previously sensitized to FD&C Yellow No. 5 Aluminium Lake/CI 19140.

Product conforms to EN71, ASTM F-963-11, ASTM D4236 safety requirements and all applicable CPSC and CPSIA standards.
No lead or phthalate hazard.

TOP TATTOOS

Tattoo artists are extremely talented—some of the boys' intricate designs took hours to complete. See for yourself—copy Harry's butterfly tattoo using the grid lines to help you.

TOTALLY CHARMING

How many 1D charm bracelets are tangled here? Count them, and then add some charms of your own.

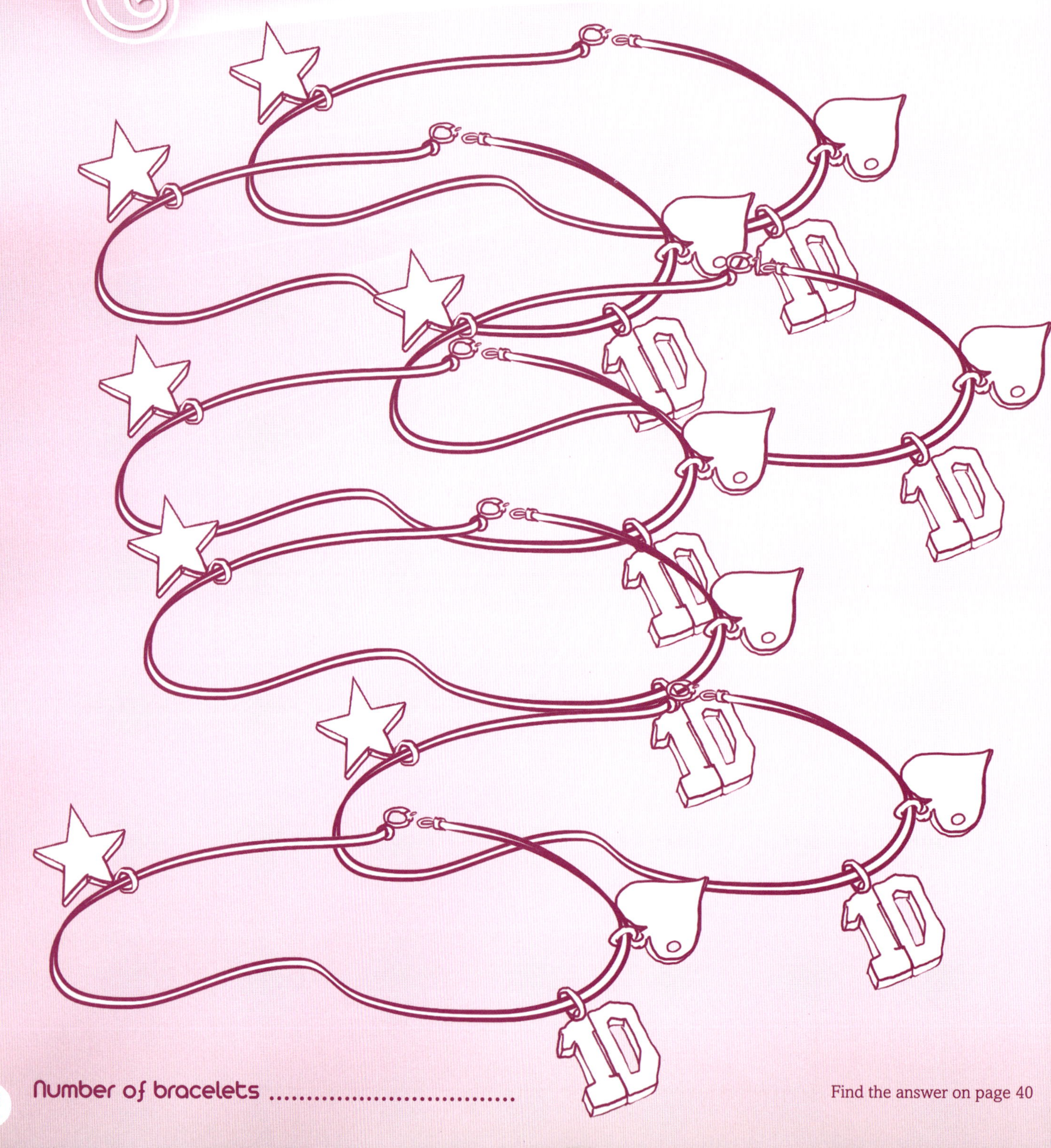

Number of bracelets ....

Find the answer on page 40

CHANNEL HOPPING

Ooh, ooh! One Direction are on TV again! Use the pictures below to copy your fave band member onto the small screen.

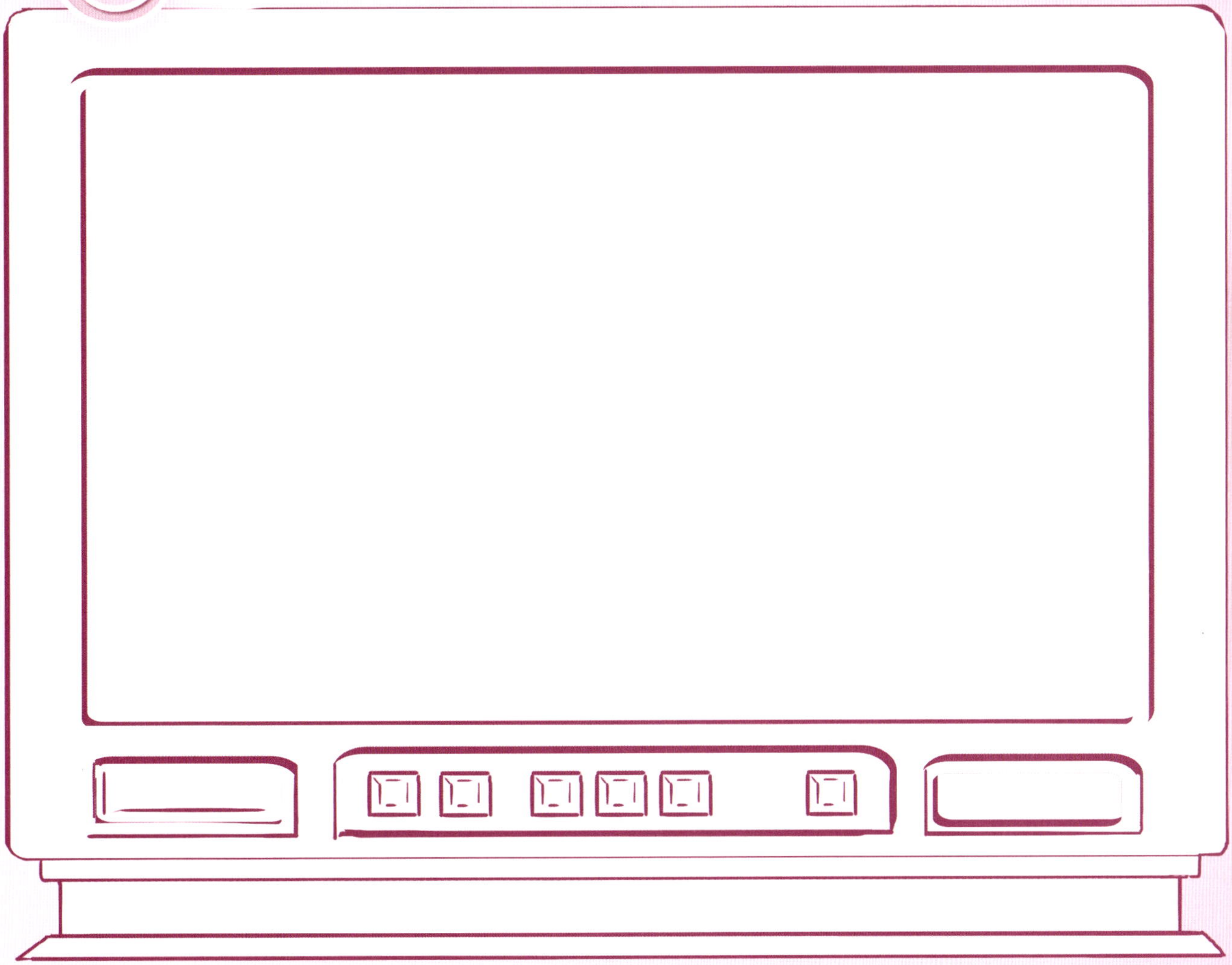

SWEET DREAMS

Shh! Harry is taking a nap! What do you think he is dreaming about?

CUSTOM-MADE

Customize your sneakers in a 1D way! Start by pinning badges to the laces (that way they won't hurt your feet). If you're allowed, use a permanent marker to copy your fave tattoos onto the sides.

Let's face it—all five members of One Direction are gorgeous, but most people have a favorite. There's no need to choose, though—with this book, you can have the best of them all!

Find the answer on page 40

HEART ATTACK

Avert your eyes from the boys for just one moment... how many heart tattoos are jumbled up? And which other 1D tattoos can you spot in there?

C'MON, C'MON

Shade in any square that has the letters C'MON to reveal a hidden 1D song title. Do you know which album it's from?

C	M	O	N	C	O	N	C
O	M	H	N	M	C	O	N
C	M	C	M	O	A	N	M
P	M	O	O	N	C	C	O
N	O	C	M	P	M	O	O
C	I	N	O	O	N	M	N
M	C	O	N	O	M	L	C
O	C	Y	M	M	O	N	O

Find the answers on page 40

He's the level-headed, mature member of the band—sound like your type of guy?

Liam Payne

BIRTHPLACE: Wolverhampton (England)

BIRTH DATE: August 29, 1993

ASTROLOGICAL SIGN: Virgo

PARENTS: Mom Karen; dad Geoff

HOBBIES: Boxing, surfing

LIKES TO LISTEN TO: Justin Timberlake, Usher, Gary Barlow, Kanye West, Jay-Z, Ed Sheeran

FAVE COLOR: Purple

FAVE COUNTRY: Ghana

LOOK OUT FOR: His over-riding enthusiasm—his favorite words are "brilliant" and "fantastic"

THINGS THAT MAKE HIM GO "OOGH": Super-spicy food

THINGS THAT MAKE HIM GO "MMMM": Cheesy potato chips, chocolate

TOP TATTOOS: Feather on his inner arm; "only time will tell" on his wrist; four arrows on his right arm

ODD ONE OUT

How well do you know Liam's likes and dislikes? Spot the odd one out here—it's a tricky one!

Find the answer on page 40

DID YOU KNOW?

★ Liam was bullied at school, so he takes an active role in anti-bullying campaigns.

★ He says that out of all the boys, he's "the clumsy one."

★ At school, he would get up early to go long-distance running!

FACE IN THE CROWD

So, you think you'd know Liam anywhere? See if you can spot him in the crowd at this sports game!

LOGICAL LIAM

Liam and Niall are trying to find out who is in each dressing room, and what has been left outside. Help!

Louis is one floor down from Zayn.

Harry isn't on the first floor, but has a gold star on his door.

The person on the second floor has flowers outside his door.

Food has been left outside one room, and drinks outside another.

The room on the first floor has a silver star. It doesn't have drinks outside.

The boy on the third floor is directly above the person with a bronze star.

Find the answers on page 40

	Which floor?	Star color?	What's outside?
Harry			
Zayn			
Louis			

One Direction is without a doubt the greatest boy band EVER! Don't forget—they're fabuLouis, phenomiNiall, amaZayn, brilLiam, and extraordinHarry—and you know it!

MORE THAN THIS

How many words can you make from this song off the *Take Me Home* album?

CHANGE MY MIND

dance

Find the answers on page 40

OVER AGAIN

There are too many letters here! Cross out the surplus letters from each line to reveal one of the songs performed at the *X Factor* bootcamp stage. Do you know who chose it?

HSHHTOHPH ....

CARAYIANAG ....

PYPOPURP ....

SHESASRTS ....

MMOMUMTM ....

Find the answers on page 40

Find the answer on page 40

BEST DRESSED

Take some style tips from these notoriously clothes-savvy superstars…

SAME MISTAKES

Something is wrong in this picture—can you see what it is?

STORY OF MY LIFE

Do you know who this is?

My surname was originally Austin but I took my stepdad's name later on. I was born on Christmas Eve and used to work at my local movie theater.

Find the answer on page 40

We would—would you?! Of course! That's to say, we would listen to 1D whenever possible, learn everything about them, and TOTALLY love it if we got the chance to spend time with them!

HALF A HEART

Uh-oh! The last thing we want is broken hearts. Can you match these up to make them better again?

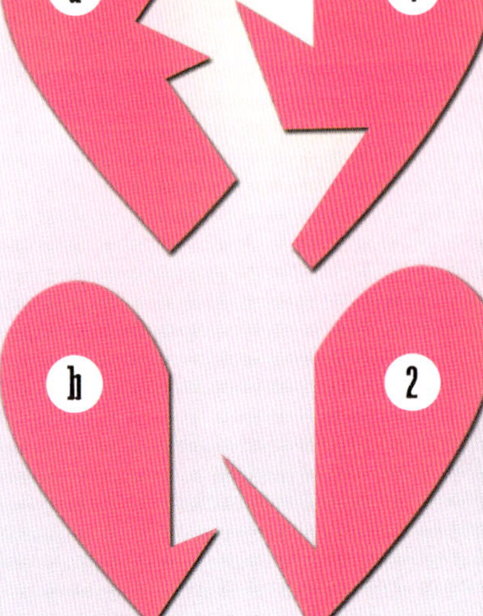

c
3

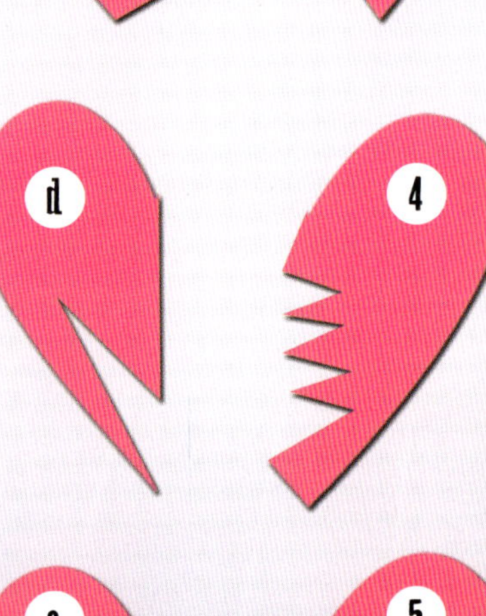

ONE THING

Can you find **THING** hidden just once in this grid?

G	I	H	T	N	T	H	I	N	N	G	I
I			T	H	I	G	N	I	G	I	N
N			H	I	I	T	T			T	T
G	T	H	I	N	T	N	H			H	H
T	I	N	N	T	H	I	I	N	G	I	G
H	T	G			I	H	I	T	N	N	T
I	H	T			N	I	I	H			N
N	G	I	H	T	G	T	H	G			I
H	N	I	N	T			C	N	H	I	H
H	I	T	H	I			O	N	I	H	T

Find the answers on page 40

THROUGH THE DARK

?

Who is this hiding in the shadows?

....

COVER UP

Cut out all the magazine pics you can find of the boys, and you'll soon have enough to create a collage to cover your notebooks. Simply lay them out, overlapping slightly so there are no gaps at all, and glue them in place. Take time to arrange them first so you know they will fit. Start at one corner and work across, or place a larger picture in the middle and work out to the edges.

BETTER THAN WORDS

Use the decoder to figure out what this banner says!

☼	●	✝	❖	👍	⇦	✏	★
A	B	E	F	G	H	I	L

💧	▲	♫	👄	⏭	🚹	📻	⬆
N	O	R	T	U	V	W	Y

....

....

Find the answers on page 40

NIALL'S PAGE

Find out the secrets of the band's blondie—such a cutie, too!

Niall Horan

BIRTHPLACE: Mullingar, County Westmeath (Ireland)

BIRTH DATE: September 13, 1993

ASTROLOGICAL SIGN: Virgo

PARENTS: Mom Maura; dad Bobby; stepdad Chris

HOBBIES: Eating, watching TV

LIKES TO LISTEN TO: Coldplay, Oasis, Michael Bublé, Bon Jovi, The Eagles

FAVE COLOR: Green

FAVE COUNTRY: Australia

LOOK OUT FOR: The amount of noise he makes—he's usually heard before he's seen!

THINGS THAT MAKE HIM GO "OOGH": Birds and clowns

THINGS THAT MAKE HIM GO "MMMM": Pizza, muffins, potatoes—food in general!

TOP TATTOOS: None

mmmm!

Why was the clown sad?

He broke his funny bone!

FAMOUS FRIENDS

Which one of these celebs is NOT known for being friendly with Niall?

Find the answer on page 40

NAILED IT!

Paint your nails for Niall! Luckily, he has just the right number of letters in his name for you to write ILOVENIALL across your fingers. Start with a pale base coat and when it is completely dry, use a cocktail stick or nail painting tools to make tiny dots spelling out the words in a darker nail polish. If you prefer, you can paint I♥1D across your fingers, or arrows and hearts in your fave colors.

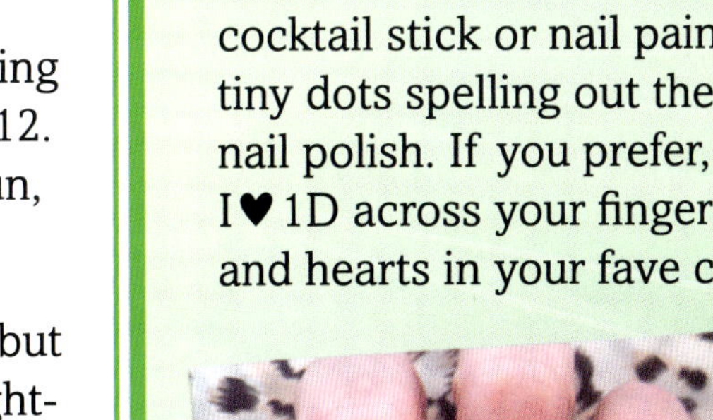

DID YOU KNOW?

★ Niall has been dyeing his hair since he was 12. Blondes have more fun, after all!

★ He is left-handed, but he plays the guitar right-handed.

★ His suggestion for the band's name was Niall and the Potatoes. Catchy!

GUITAR MAN

Can you spot three differences between these two pictures?

Find the answer on page 40

One of them—or more—must have stolen your heart. Go on, confess—who's your favorite?

LITTLE WHITE LIES

Which of these are true, and which are teeny weeny fibs?

1. Harry and Liam are the only two members who have passed their driving test. T F
2. Zayn is a huge hip hop and R&B fan. T F
3. Harry's a clever guy—before he was in the band, he wanted to be a doctor. T F
4. Niall is an uncle! He has a nephew named Theo T F
5. The song "I Want" was written by Tom Fletcher from McFly. T F
6. Liam has a reputation for being the perfectionist in the band. T F
7. The name One Direction was Harry's idea. T F
8. Niall is scared of pigeons after one flew in while he was in the bathroom. T F
9. "Live While We're Young" appears on the *Up All Night* album. T F
10. The band has appeared on Sesame Street, bigging up the letter U. T F

Find the answers on page 40

GOTTA BE YOU

Who's hiding underneath these disguises?

....

Find the answers on page 40

APRIL FOOLS

The boys aren't averse to playing tricks on each other. Who pulled these pranks, and on whom? Fill in the blanks and try not to laugh too hard…

__________ **shaved his initials on the leg hair of** __________

__________ **pulled down the pants of** __________ **at a burger joint**

__________ **and** __________ **hired an actress to pretend she was having a baby and shock** __________

Find the answers on page 40

STORY OF MY LIFE

Do you know who's describing himself here?

I have one older sister and two younger sisters. I have both my ears pierced, and I always brush my teeth before I go on stage!

....

Find the answer on page 40

AMAZING ART

You can create your own amazing art, even if you're not great at drawing. Find a black and white picture of one or all of the boys—one that's not too small. Place tracing paper over the top and you'll be able to see the outlines and shadows that form the faces. Just draw around the main outlines with a pencil to capture the basic image, and color it in. It should look stunning—and unique!

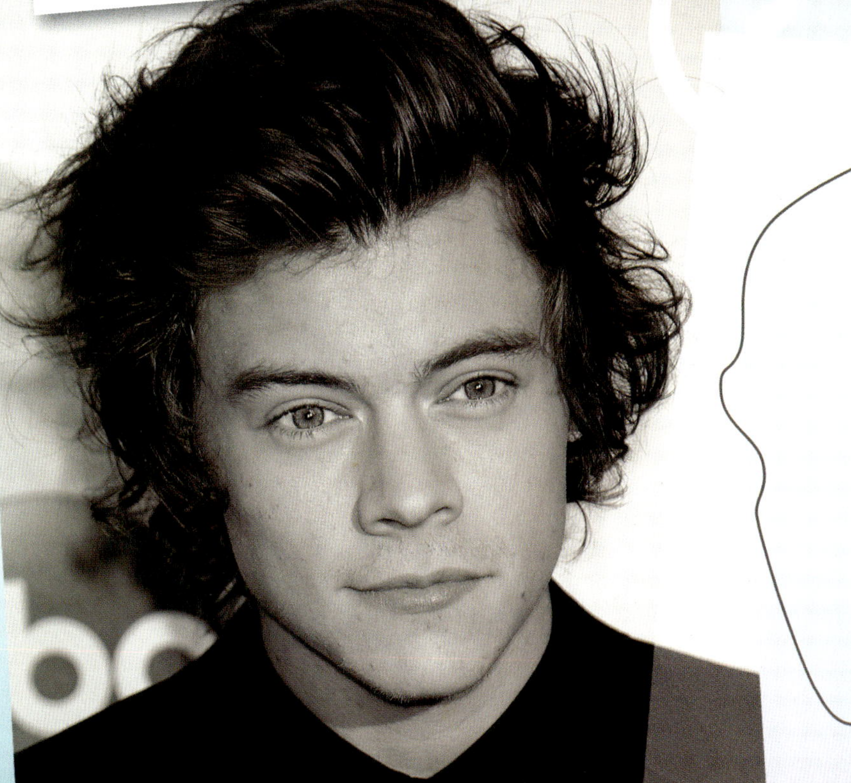

We left the youngest until last—did you wait patiently or flip to the end?

Harry Styles

BIRTHPLACE: Holmes Chapel, Cheshire (England)

BIRTH DATE: February 1, 1994

ASTROLOGICAL SIGN: Aquarius

PARENTS: Mom Anne; dad Des; stepdad Robin

HOBBIES: Fashion, art, tennis, badminton, surfing

LIKES TO LISTEN TO: The Beatles, Elvis Presley, Coldplay, Adele

FAVE COLORS: Blue and orange

FAVE COUNTRY: England

LOOK OUT FOR: His trademark look of skinny jeans and a blazer or dressed-down hoody and beanie

THINGS THAT MAKE HIM GO "OOGH": Swearing, olives, beetroot

THINGS THAT MAKE HIM GO "MMMM": Apple juice, sweet corn, tacos

TOP TATTOOS: Butterfly under his pecs; pirate ship on left bicep; pair of birds on his collarbone

THE OLDEN DAYS

Believe it or not, Harry was in another band before One Direction came on the scene. Use the grid code to find out what they were called.

c3.a4.b1.d2.b3

b3.c1.a2.b1.d4.a3

	1	2	3	4
a	B	K	O	H
b	I	D	E	L
c	S	N	W	P
d	Y	T	A	M

....

....

Find the answer on page 40

DID YOU KNOW?

★ Harry loves animals, especially rabbits, cats, dogs, and hamsters—but his faves are turtles!

★ He can juggle and play the kazoo. Such talents!

★ He's a big softie and likes girly films like *Love Actually* and *Titanic*.

HARRY'S HERO

Follow the tangled lines to find which of these people is Harry's hero.

A: David Hasselhoff

B: President Obama

C: Tom Cruise

Find the answer on page 40

ONE AND ONLY

There's only one Harry Styles! Can you find the name HARRY hidden just once in this grid?

R	A	Y	H	A	R	A	Y
H	R	Y	H	A	Y	R	R
A	H	Y	H	A	R	R	H
R	A	H	A	H	R	A	H
R	H	A	R	Y	A	R	R
R	Y	R	H	R	Y	Y	Y
Y	R	A	H	H	A	R	R
A	A	R	A	Y	R	Y	A

Find the answer on page 40

We've nearly reached the end—do you know more about the boys than ever before?

1D IN NUMBERS

Don't worry, there's no math involved—but you do need to be a 1D know-it-all. Fill in the blanks with the numbers in the stars below.

2014 2 12 17 7 2008 12 3 12

The year three of the band members turned 21

....

Number of countries where their debut album was number 1

....

The year Liam first auditioned on *X Factor*

....

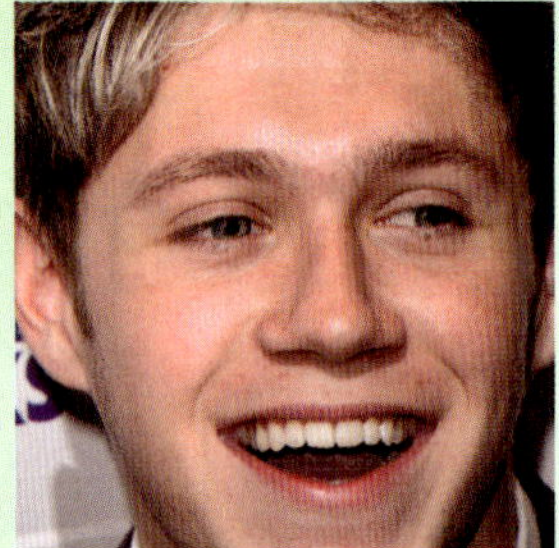

Total number 1 albums in the U.S. in 2012

....

The number of times they sing "crazy" in "Live While We're Young"

....

The series of *X Factor* where the band was formed

....

The number on the clock for their third album

....

The band's final position on *X Factor*

....

The height in inches of each 1D official doll

....

Find the answers on page 40

KISS YOU-DOKU

Fill in the blanks so that there's one of each symbol in every row, column, and mini-grid.

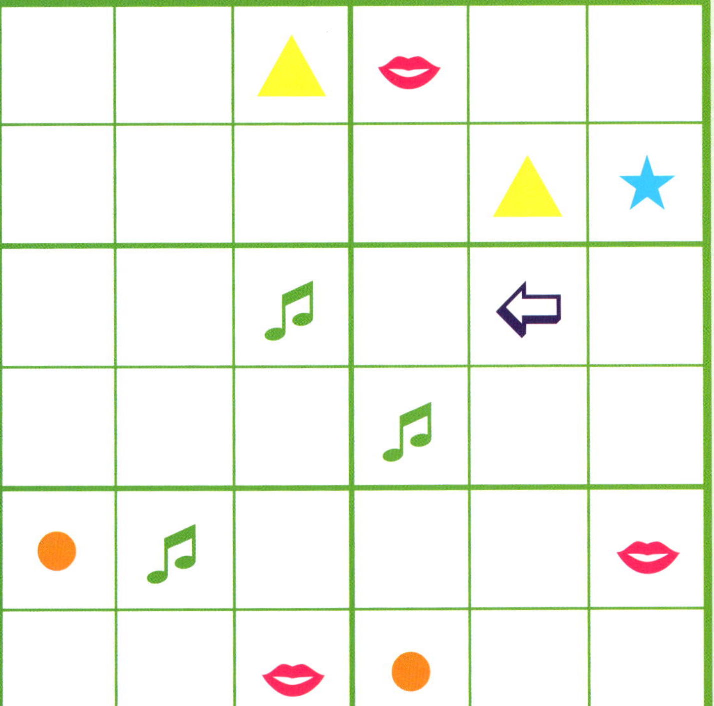

WEAR IT WELL

Here's a 1D bracelet you can make for all your friends so that you're bound together in your love of the fabulous five. All you need are embroidery threads in five different shades.

★ Cut a 20-inch (50-cm) length of each thread and place them all together.

★ Hold one end between your teeth while you twist the loose end around and around really tightly for the whole length. Hold the end to prevent it from untwisting, and place one finger in the middle.

★ Fold it in half, placing both ends together, and the whole thing will twist around itself.

★ Tie a large knot to hold it together, and add five beads on the loose ends if you like.

CROSS OUT

There are too many letters here! Cross out every other letter, starting with "S," to reveal a song the boys have fun with at their live shows.

TSEHEINRANGKEDDWICRYTPBSALG

Find the answer on page 40

Find the answer on page 40

Page 5
WHOSE TATTOO? 1. Louis; 2. Harry; 3. Louis; 4. Zayn; 5. Harry; 6. Zayn; 7. Liam; 8. Louis; 9. Zayn; 10. Harry.

Page 7
MATCHMAKING Liam James Payne, Wolverhampton; Harry Edward Styles, Holmes Chapel, Cheshire; Louis William Tomlinson, Doncaster; Niall James Horan, Mullingar; Zayn Javadd Malik, Bradford.

BEST BAND EVER

Page 8
TELL ME A LIE Niall is fibbing—it was Liam who dropped the laptop and broke his own toe causing him "Payne" (ha ha!).

WHERE WE ARE 1. Toronto; 2. Miami; 3. Mexico City; 4. Santiago; 5. Rio de Janeiro; 6. Buenos Aires; 7. Dublin; 8. Manchester; 9. Paris; 10. Copenhagen; 11. Tokyo; 12. Brisbane; 13. Auckland.

Page 9
STORY OF MY LIFE Harry

Page 11
FEELING ODD D

CALL ME LOU? Robbo, Mr. Pinkerton, Lolly Bolly, and Brian are made up. Hee hee!

Page 12
STORY OF MY LIFE Niall

THROUGH THE DARK Zayn

NAME THAT TUNE 1. "Tell me a lie"; 2. "Better than words"; 3. "Change my mind"; 4. "Through the dark"; 5. "They don't know about us"; 6. "Back for you"; 7. "Everything about you"; 8. "Don't forget where you belong."

Page 13
ONE DIRECTION

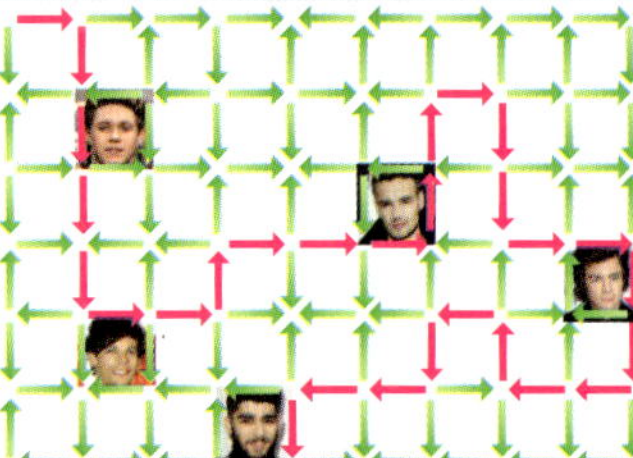

Page 15
ZAYN'S MAZE Zayn's fave animal is a lion.

PUPPY LOVE Tonto

Page 16
STORY OF MY LIFE Liam

MORE THAN THIS You can find these words, and many more: ghost, dirt, memoir, items, home, indigo, modest, resting, remote, storm...

IN PIECES C

Page 17
LIVE PERFORMANCE

Page 18
MATCHMAKING
"We're not perfect, we're not clean cut. We're trying to be ourselves." = Louis
"If it were legal, I'd marry food." = Niall
"My trademark saying is probably 'VAS HAPPENIN?!'" = Zayn
"My sister used to call me Cheesy Head because I loved these cheesy crisps." = Liam
"I hope that I'd still be touring with One Direction in ten years' time. I love this job so much—if you need to call it a job." = Harry

Page 19
HANGING AROUND It's Niall, just chilling with his guitar.

Page 20
FOLLOWING FASHION C

Page 22
TOTALLY CHARMING 7 bracelets

Page 25
HEART ATTACK There are 23 heart tattoos plus Harry's bird and Louis's stick figure.

THROUGH THE DARK Harry

C'MON, C'MON The hidden song is "HAPPILY" from the album *Midnight Memories.*

PAGE 26
ODD ONE OUT Liam likes them all except for spoons—he has a weird phobia about them!

Page 27
FACE IN THE CROWD

LOGICAL LIAM
Harry is on the third floor with a gold star and drinks outside his room.
Zayn is on the second floor, with a bronze star on the door and flowers outside.
Louis is on the first floor with a silver star and food outside.

Page 28
MORE THAN THIS You can find these words, and lots of others: niche, named, head, dice, denim, cinema, aimed, candy, chimney, magic.

OVER AGAIN STOP CRYING YOUR HEART OUT. Liam and Harry both sang the Oasis song on *X Factor.*

Page 29
SAME MISTAKES Lol—look at Niall's footwear!

STORY OF MY LIFE Louis

Page 30
ONE THING

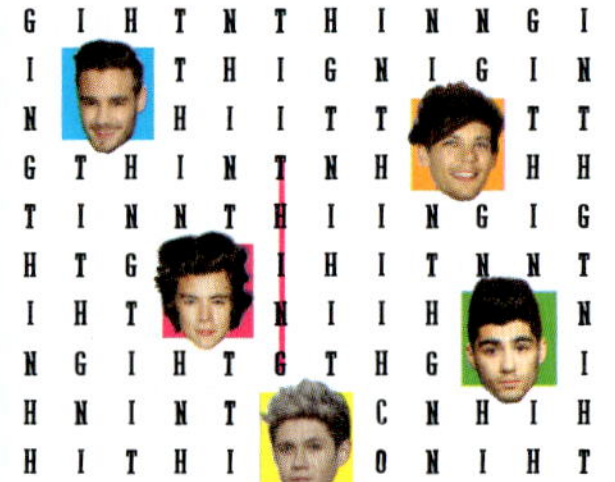

HALF A HEART a = 3, b = 5, c = 4, d = 2, e = 1

Page 31
THROUGH THE DARK Niall

BETTER THAN WORDS "Live while we're young"

Page 33
FAMOUS FRIENDS He's not known for being friends with Cheryl Cole.

GUITAR MAN

Page 34
LITTLE WHITE LIES 1. False; 2. True; 3. False; 4. True; 5. True; 6. False; 7. True; 8. True; 9. False; 10. True.

GOTTA BE YOU a. Niall; b. Louis; c. Liam; d. Harry; e. Zayn.

Page 35
APRIL FOOLS Harry shaved his initials on the leg hair of Zayn. Liam pulled down the pants of Niall at a burger joint. Zayn and Louis hired an actress to pretend she was having a baby and shock Harry.

STORY OF MY LIFE Zayn

Page 37
THE OLDEN DAYS Harry's band was called WHITE ESKIMO.

HARRY'S HEROES
A: David Hasselhoff

ONE AND ONLY

R A Y H A R A Y
H R Y H A Y R R
A H Y H A R R H
R A H A H R A H
R H A R Y A R R
R Y R H R Y Y Y
Y R A H H A R R
A A R A Y R Y A

Page 38
1D IN NUMBERS The year three of the band members turned 21 = 2014; Number of countries where their debut album was number 1 = 17; The year Liam first auditioned on *X Factor* = 2008; Total number 1 albums in the U.S. in 2012 = 2; The number of times they sing "crazy" in "Live While We're Young" = 12; The series of *X Factor* where the band was formed = 7; The number on the clock for their third album = 12; The band's final position on *X Factor* = 3; The height in inches of each 1D official doll = 12

page 39
KISS YOU-DOKU

CROSS OUT
"TEENAGE DIRTBAG"

THROUGH THE DARK Liam